The Story of Flight

WEIRD & WONDERFUL AIRCRAFT

Crabtree Publishing Company
www.crabtreebooks.com

PMB 16A, 350 Fifth Avenue,
Suite 3308
New York, NY 10118

612 Welland Avenue
St. Catharines, Ontario
L2M 5V6

Published in 2004 by
Crabtree Publishing Company

Coordinating editor: Ellen Rodger
Project editors: Sean Charlebois, Carrie Gleason
Production coordinator: Rose Gowsell

Created and Produced by
David West ⚇ Children's Books

Project Development, Design, and Concept
David West Children's Books:
Designer: Rob Shone
Editor: Gail Bushnell
Illustrators: James Field, Mike Lacey & Stephen Sweet
(SGA), Gary Slater & Steve Weston (Specs Art), Alain
Salesse (Contact Jupiter)
Picture Research: Carlotta Cooper

Photo Credits:
Abbreviations: t-top, m-middle, b-bottom, r-right,
l-left, c-center.

Front cover & pages 6t, 14t & b, 16t & b, 20, 23t,
24t, 28b - The Flight Collection. 6b - Library of
Congress. 9, 18, 19 - The Culture Archive. 10, 13 -
Royal Air Force Museum. 11 - @ 1996 EAA/Jim
Koepnick. 21, 23b, 24b, 27t, 28t - NASA. 25 -
Corbis Images. 27b - Rex Features.

06 05 04 03
10 9 8 7 6 5 4 3 2 1

Printed and bound in Dubai

Library of Congress Cataloging-in-Publication Data
Hansen, Ole Steen.
   Weird and wonderful aircraft/ written by Ole Steen Hansen.
      p. cm. -- (The story of flight)
Includes index.
Contents: Ups and downs -- Massive multiplanes -- German oddities
-- Twins -- Piston power -- Little and large -- Flying hybrids -- Speed --
VTOL -- Flying wings -- Muscle power -- Canards.
ISBN 0-7787-1210-9 (RLB : alk. paper) -- ISBN 0-7787-1226-5 (PB :
alk. paper)
   1. Research aircraft--Juvenile literature. [1. Research aircraft. 2.
Airplanes.] I. Title.
II. Series.
   TL567.R47H36 2003
   629.133--dc22
                                                      2003016178

The Story of Flight

WEIRD & WONDERFUL AIRCRAFT

Ole Steen Hansen

U S AIR FORCE

 Crabtree Publishing Company
www.crabtreebooks.com

CONTENTS

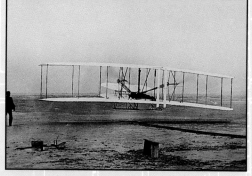

HISTORIC BEGINNINGS
Orville and Wilbur Wright designed, built, and flew the world's first powered aircraft, the Wright *Flyer*, in 1903. The basic principles of flight used by the Wright brothers are still used by aircraft designers today.

BACK TO THE DRAWING BOARD
All new aircraft start as ideas in the minds of their designers. Plans are drawn up and then aircraft are built and test flown. After that, it is back to the drawing board to perfect the design. Sometimes the drawings are just thrown in the trash!

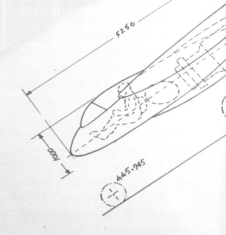

INTRODUCTION

SUCCESS STORY

The Boeing 747 was a risky design project because of its big size. Designers wondered whether airlines would buy such a big jet and whether there would be enough passengers to fill the seats. The 747 turned out to be a success story. It helped make air travel so cheap that today many people can afford to fly.

A ircraft designers are always coming up with new, and sometimes strange, designs for "flying machines." Some designs work and some do not. Occasionally, old designs are altered to make new aircraft. Designers must understand the scientific principles of flight in order to create a safe aircraft. This book has a wide selection of unusual, daring, and sometimes utterly strange ideas, which show the amazing variety of aircraft in the world.

UPS AND DOWNS

The pioneers of flight were up against heavy odds. They had to teach themselves to fly and test their new designs at the same time. No wonder they sometimes crashed!

A.V. ROE

Alliot Verdon Roe won money in a model aircraft contest in 1907. This made it possible for him to start designing full size aircraft. He was so short of money that his 1909 triplane was built under a row of railway arches in North London, U.K. It was covered in packing paper, instead of fabric.

Phillips' Multiplane

Before the Wright brothers flew, Horatio Phillips, the son of a London gunsmith, discovered that long, narrow wings were best for flight. This is why modern sailplanes have such long wings. Phillips had no success making a practical aircraft. On his 1907 design, he had 200 narrow wings arranged in four frames. Amazingly it actually took off, but only flew a few feet.

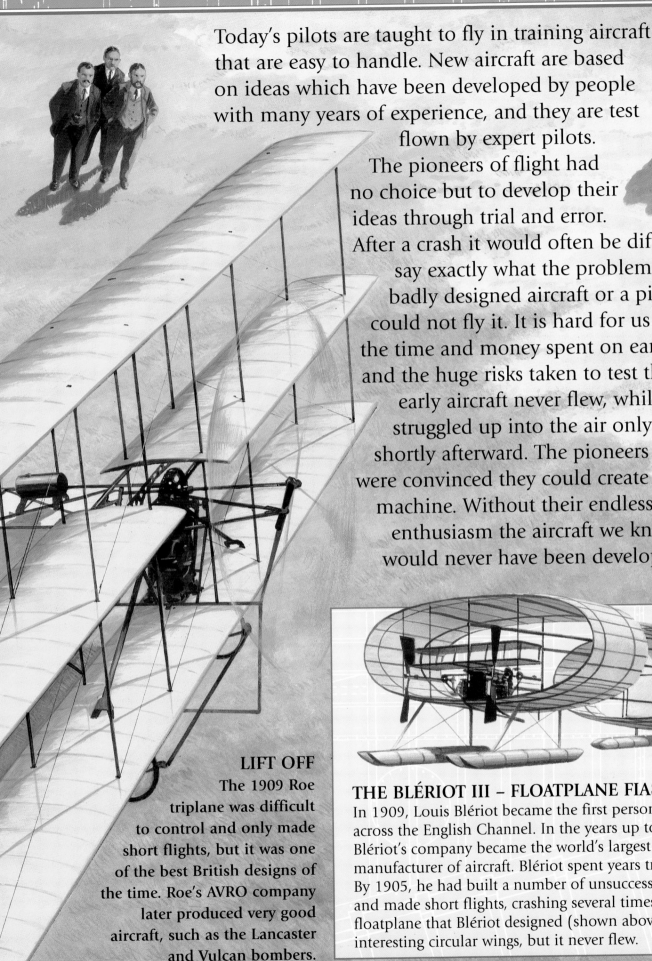

Today's pilots are taught to fly in training aircraft that are easy to handle. New aircraft are based on ideas which have been developed by people with many years of experience, and they are test flown by expert pilots. The pioneers of flight had no choice but to develop their ideas through trial and error. After a crash it would often be difficult to say exactly what the problem was: a badly designed aircraft or a pilot who could not fly it. It is hard for us to imagine the time and money spent on early designs and the huge risks taken to test them. Some early aircraft never flew, while others struggled up into the air only to crash shortly afterward. The pioneers of flight were convinced they could create a flying machine. Without their endless enthusiasm the aircraft we know today would never have been developed.

LIFT OFF
The 1909 Roe triplane was difficult to control and only made short flights, but it was one of the best British designs of the time. Roe's AVRO company later produced very good aircraft, such as the Lancaster and Vulcan bombers.

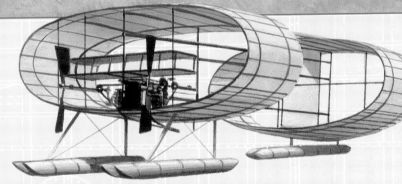

THE BLÉRIOT III – FLOATPLANE FIASCO
In 1909, Louis Blériot became the first person ever to fly across the English Channel. In the years up to 1914, Blériot's company became the world's largest manufacturer of aircraft. Blériot spent years trying to fly. By 1905, he had built a number of unsuccessful aircraft and made short flights, crashing several times. The 1906 floatplane that Blériot designed (shown above) had interesting circular wings, but it never flew.

MASSIVE MULTIPLANES

Many early aircraft were biplanes because two wings braced by struts and wires proved stronger than one. Early aircraft designers also decided that several wings were better than one for increasing the lift of an aircraft.

Some huge and heavy multiplanes, or planes with multiple wings, were designed after **World War I**. Italian Count Gianni Caproni wanted to create the world's largest airliner, capable of flying 100 passengers over the Atlantic Ocean. He calculated that nine wings were needed for his Ca-60 Transaereo flying boat. In England, designer Walter Barling created the Tarrant Tabor triplane bomber.

GIANNI CAPRONI
Count Gianni Caproni was a man who "thought big." His company built huge triplane bombers during World War I, but the crash of the nine-winged Ca-60 Transaereo ended Caproni's transatlantic flight dreams forever.

The Tarrant Tabor triplane crashed on take-off. After this fiasco, Barling traveled to the United States and convinced some air force officers that he could build them a bomber for future wars. Barling's plane, the Barling Bomber, was almost too heavy to fly. In the early 1920s it was still not possible to build successful aircraft that lived up to the dreams of these men. One problem was the lack of powerful engines.

MULTIPLANE MADNESS
The Ca-60 was built from wood, had eight engines and a luxurious cabin for its 100 passengers. Only the test pilot ever flew in it, as it crashed shortly after take-off on its first flight.

Barling Bomber
The six-engined Barling Bomber was first flown in 1923. It was so heavy that the crew had to choose between fuel or bombs. Small amounts of both could be carried, but then the monster triplane could only hit targets located nearby with a light bomb load. It was hardly a bomber that would make the enemy panic. Only one was built and it was destroyed by fire in 1928.

GAX
The American GAX triplane was intended to bombard enemy **trenches** during World War I. Unfortunately, the GAX design was not completed before the war ended in 1918. The GAX had nine guns and heavy armor plating to protect the three man crew and its engines. The aircraft was too heavy for the two 400 horsepower engines. The GAX flew slowly, but never very well. Later armored ground attack aircraft, like today's A-10, played important roles in warfare.

GERMAN ODDITIES

During World War II German designers made many new and innovative aircraft. Some were driven by propellers, others by jet, or rocket engines. Some looked just like science fiction creations.

HANNA REITSCH
Test pilot Hanna Reitsch flew a special version of the Fi 103 to find out why the type crashed. She solved the problems and later promoted the idea of using the Fi 103 as a suicide attack aircraft.

FI 103
Length: 26 ft 3 in (8 m)
Wingspan: 18 ft 9 in (5.7 m)
Speed: 404 mph (650 km/h)

The Fi 103 was a manned suicide version of the unmanned V-1 flying bomb. There were 173 Fi 103s built, but the suicide attack project was canceled before any missions were flown.

BACHEM BA 349A (NATTER)
Length: 20 ft (6.1 m)
Wingspan: 11 ft 10 in (3.6 m)
Speed: 497 mph (800 km/h)

The Ba 349 Natter was a vertically launched rocket fighter. It was intended to climb quickly to attack Allied bombers with rockets fired from the nose.

Germany lost World War II, but throughout the war years their designers tried desperately to come up with aircraft that would help them win the war. Many designers felt they were helping defend their homeland during war. Some of the country's best scientists and **engineers** worked on aircraft design projects.

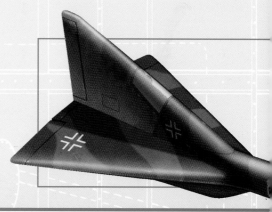

German industry could not turn all of their new ideas into military aircraft. Some designs were very good, while others were disastrous. One bad idea was the Ba 349A Natter rocket fighter, which was first tested without a pilot. When it was finally tried with a pilot, it nosedived straight into the ground from a height of over 4,921 feet (1,500 meters), killing the pilot. The war ended soon after, so it never flew in combat.

Burt Rutan's Boomerang

The Boomerang designed by Burt Rutan in the 1990s is an **asymmetrical** aircraft, like the BV 141. It looks like it could not possibly fly in a straight line, but it handles better than many ordinary twin-engined aircraft. It uses a laptop computer for **navigation**.

BV 141

Length: 45 ft 9 in (14 m)
Wingspan: 57 ft 4 in (17.5 m)
Speed: 230 mph (370 km/h)

The world's most asymmetrical airplane was developed as an observation aircraft. It actually flew quite well, but pilots did not like the weird look of it and not many were built.

SACK AS-6 V1

Length: 21 ft (6.4 m)
Wingspan: 16 ft 5 in (5 m)

The AS-6 was developed from a model aircraft flown by Arthur Sack in 1939. The AS-6 was built from wood and had the engine and nose parts of a Me 108 touring aircraft. It looked funny and never flew.

COAL POWER

On the Lippisch 13A the cockpit was in the tail fin. The jet fighter was supposed to be powered by coal dust and reach twice the speed of sound. An unpowered glider version was built for test flying.

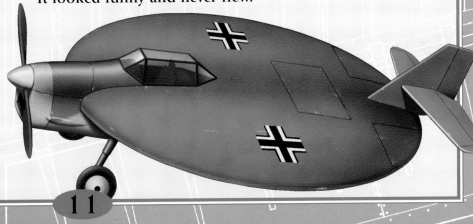

TWINS

Some of the strangest aircraft in the history of aviation were called twin types. During World War II twin types were made by joining two aircraft into a new, bigger plane.

CUB DUO
The Piper Cub has been a popular light plane since the 1930s. Harold Wagner of Portland, Oregon, liked flying Cubs so much that he decided to join two fuselages together and build his own unique Twin Cub.

YO+GD

DOUBLE TROUBLE – HE 111Z
The pilot flew the He 111Z from the port (left) fuselage. The second pilot doubled as a navigator in the starboard (right) fuselage. There were five other crew members, including the mechanics, gunners, and a radio operator.

In Germany, the Messerschmitt company produced the huge Me 321 "Gigant" cargo glider. It had a wingspan almost as big as a Boeing 747 Jumbojet and it could transport 200 soldiers or a tank. The only problem was that the German air force did not have a plane powerful enough to tow it into the air! Three Bf 110 fighters tried successfully but this was not a safe option. The solution was to build a dedicated tow plane by turning two twin-engined Heinkel He 111 bombers into the He 111Z – the Z stood for the German word "Zwilling" which means "twin." The fuselages were joined by a central section wing with three engines. The five-engined tow plane had plenty of power and the twelve built were very popular with their crews.

MESSERSCHMITT BF 109Z

In Germany a heavy fighter was designed by joining two Bf 109 fighters. The Bf 109Z was the result. It was a single seater with the pilot sitting in the left fuselage. The Bf 109Z would have been heavily armed with five 30 mm canons. Four versions were planned, but only one prototype was built in 1942–43. The project was canceled because a new jet fighter, the Messerschmitt Me 262, was expected to perform better.

Twin Mustang

The P-82 Twin Mustang was intended as a long range, or distance, fighter for the war over the Pacific during World War II. It looked like the P-51 Mustang, but it was more than two Mustangs joined together. Few Twin Mustangs were built before World War II ended. They were used by the U.S. Air Force during the **Korean War**. The night fighter version (shown at left) had radar mounted under the central wing.

PISTON POWER

Piston engines powered the huge aircraft that were designed and built during World War II. They seemed to be good ideas but by the time they were completed nobody wanted them.

The eight-engined HK-1 Hercules flying boat had a wingspan as large as a Boeing 747 Jumbojet and a B-17 Flying Fortress combined! It was built to fly troops, tanks, and equipment over the Atlantic, but the threat from German **U-boats** during World War II was over by the time the HK-1 finally took off on its only flight in 1947. A second big aircraft idea, the British-built Bristol Brabazon, could fly 100 passengers non-stop from New York to London.

HOWARD HUGHES

The HK-1 was the brainchild of billionaire pilot and aircraft designer, Howard Hughes. He helped design some very advanced aircraft, but the HK-1 was hopelessly outdated, even before its first flight.

JUNKERS G 38

When the German Junkers G 38 took off in 1929 it was the largest civilian land plane ever constructed. It carried up to 34 passengers, who could walk inside the wing and enjoy the view from windows in the leading edge.

The captain would leave the controls with the second-in-command and walk around talking to his passengers. Only two G 38s were built, but they were flown on routes all over Europe.

SPRUCE GOOSE
The HK-1 was built from wood and earned the nickname "Spruce Goose." In fact, most of it was built from birch, carefully selected from forests in the U.S.A. and Canada.

WING AND ENGINES
In 1949, the Bristol Brabazon became the largest aircraft ever to fly from a runway. Eight engines were grouped together to drive four **contra-rotating** propellers, but the Brabazon still did not have enough power. The thick wing made it possible for the Brabazon to take off at low speed from a short runway, but it was a very slow airliner.

A few years after its first flight in 1949, jets could fly more passengers at twice the speed, so the Brabazon was outdated. It cost $19,964,557 to develop and was scrapped for $15,972.

NX37602

LITTLE AND LARGE

Throughout aviation history bombers have always needed an escort of fighters to protect them against enemy aircraft. Few fighters have had the range to escort the bombers all the way to their target and back.

One solution to this problem was to have bombers carry their own fighters. In the **Soviet Union** some experiments were done with **parasite fighters** and light dive bombers in the 1930s. In the early years of the **Cold War**, from the late 1940s to the 1950s, the U.S. Air Force experimented with parasite jet fighters. The McDonnell XF-85 Goblin was designed especially for this purpose. Once its job was done, it was to be collected in mid-flight by the bomber. Unfortunately, the idea of a bomber carrying its own fighter has many disadvantages. When flying with a fighter on board, the bomber is not able to carry as many bombs or as much fuel. One fighter might not even be enough to protect the bomber. When the U.S. Air Force flew long bomber missions during the **Vietnam War** in the 1960s and 1970s they used tanker aircraft to refuel the escort fighters in-flight, giving them the range they needed.

F-84 PARASITE

When the Goblin proved difficult to put into practice, the U.S. Air Force experimented with flying F-84 Thunderjets as parasites under the mighty B-36 bombers. One squadron became operational in 1955–56, using the fighters as long range reconnaissance **aircraft**.

Airship Defense

During World War I, airships had been able to lift heavier bomb loads than any other aircraft. Airships were also prey to fighter attacks. Several experiments to launch and recover fighters from airships were conducted in Germany, Great Britain, and the United States. Gloster Grebe fighters are shown above hanging under the British Airship R-33 in 1926. By this time, the role of the airship in warfare was over and these experiments were soon stopped.

A SWARM OF PARASITES

In the Soviet Union, up to five fighters were carried around by a TB 3 bomber. Only the central fighter on the **trapeze** under the fuselage could be recovered again. Some of these aircraft were used to try to stop the invading Germans during World War II.

GOBLIN

Experiments proved that the turbulence created by the big bomber made it extremely difficult for the Goblin to hook up to it again. The Goblin also failed to match the performance levels expected of enemy fighters, so the project was abandoned.

FLYING HYBRIDS

A flying car sounds like a wacky idea but it really existed! The heyday of the roadworthy aircraft was the late 1940s, when people thought they would be the vehicles of the future.

The flying car idea was not a new one. In 1917, Glenn Curtis had built an "Autoplane," an odd-looking triplane that may or may not have flown. In the Soviet Union during World War II, O. G. Antonov suggested using wings and a twin boom tail to turn a tank into a glider. The idea was to let big aircraft tow the tank-glider behind enemy lines. The tank-gliders were then released. Once they had landed, the tank was detached from its wings and the German army would suddenly find an armored force in their midst. In the U.S. several flying cars were built, tested, and successfully flown in the 1940s and 1950s but they were not very practical.

DREAMS

Modern Mechanix & Inventions Magazine fueled dreams about everything technical and new in the 1930s. A family car autogyro graced the cover of this issue (above). Few people probably considered the large, dangerous, aerial traffic jams that would result from every family having its own flying car.

AUTOGYRO JEEPS

In Britain during World War II, a jeep with a rotor called the Rotabuggy was towed behind an aircraft. After release, it would descend with the rotor free-wheeling as an autogyro. Vehicles like jeeps and tanks were never landed this way as it was decided that they should land in big transport gliders instead.

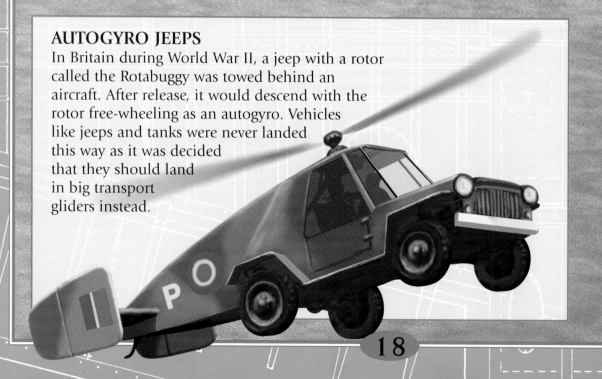

ConVair Car

The ConVair Car flew in 1946, but a later, second version ran out of fuel and crashed while attempting an emergency landing. It never went into production. Other projects were flown/driven with greater success. Unfortunately, for the price of one flying car you could buy a car that would be a better road vehicle and an aircraft that would fly more efficiently.

FLYING TANKS

The artwork here shows what might have been if the Antonov KT had been used to send tanks into battle. Control surfaces on the wings and tail unit could be operated by the tank driver/pilot, just by moving the turret.

SPEED

Aircraft designers are always trying to make faster aircraft. The first supersonic flight in the X-1 took place in 1947 and in the 1950s the quest for speed resulted in some incredibly fast supersonic aircraft.

B-58 FLYING FUEL TANK
Supersonic flight burns a great deal of fuel. The four-engined, supersonic B-58 bomber had the inside of the wing and most of the fuselage filled with fuel.

SO-9000 TRIDENT
The French SO-9000 Trident flew for the first time in 1953. It was powered by two jet engines in the wingtips and two rocket engines in the fuselage. The rocket engines were designed to provide extra boost during combat. In 1958, the Trident set an altitude record of 79,452 feet (24,217 meters). It flew at almost twice the speed of sound (Mach 2). It was a very complicated aircraft, and so the French air force soon abandoned the project.

XB-70 VALKYRIE
Design of the XB-70 began in the 1950s. One XB-70 survives in the USAF Museum near Dayton, Ohio. The other crashed in 1966 after a mid-air collision with a F-104 Starfighter.

The rocket powered X-1 had flown at supersonic speed only a few moments. Soon military jets were designed to fly at twice the speed of sound (Mach 2). There were problems with developing powerful engines and keeping the jet stable. Test flying at the time was risky. The B-58 Hustler flew in 1956 and was the first American supersonic bomber. It was designed to cross enemy airspace at high altitude to deliver its nuclear bombs. The development of anti-aircraft missiles forced the Hustler to operate at low level, where it burned up too much fuel. The B-58 also had a very short service life. The XB-70 Valkyrie was a bomber designed to fly at three times the speed of sound (Mach 3), but only two test planes were built. **Intercontinental missiles** were developed instead and became a constant nuclear threat.

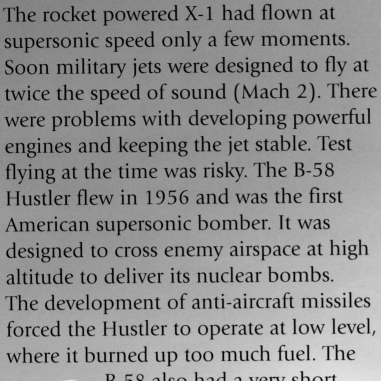

X-3 Stiletto

If there was ever an aircraft that looked fast, it was the Douglas X-3 Stiletto. Unfortunately, it was not as fast as it looked. Design of the X-3 started during World War II. It was built to explore lengthy supersonic flight and not just the short dashes expected from the first supersonic aircraft. The X-3 only managed to fly faster than the speed of sound while in a dive, because its engine was not fast enough. Its small wings also made it difficult to fly.

DANGEROUS LANDINGS

A pilot had to look over his shoulder to land the XFV-1. Test pilots practised reversing on clouds and also managed to do it on an airfield, but they considered it to be highly dangerous.

VTOL

VTOL stands for Vertical Take Off and Landing. This is no problem with a helicopter, but it is very difficult to develop a VTOL aircraft.

Military aircraft are vulnerable on the ground and the enemy can easily put them out of action by destroying their runways. For many years, aircraft designers tried to develop a combat aircraft that could take off and land vertically. A VTOL would need no runway and it could land and hide almost anywhere. The Lockheed XFV-1 was one such experimental VTOL aircraft. The take-off was successful, but landing proved so difficult that Lockheed asked the U.S. government to cancel the project. It is quite rare for an aircraft company to tell their customer that the product is that bad. Even though many later efforts were made, only one successful VTOL combat aircraft has ever been developed. It is the British Harrier, which is used by a number of different air forces. In the future, the F-35 will also come in a version with VTOL capabilities.

FLYING BEDSTEAD

In 1954, the British *Flying Bedstead* was used to demonstrate that you can balance an airframe on the exhaust of jet engines. It was not easy, but it was possible!

SHORT SC1

The Short SC1 was a VTOL research aircraft first flown in 1957. It had four engines to lift the aircraft vertically and in forward flight, while a fifth engine provided the power. It was difficult to balance the Short SC1 on the jet exhaust of the four engines because an engine failure would spell disaster. The SC1 was a useful lesson about control in hovering flight and was an essential step toward the Harrier.

Joe Walker

In the 1960s, a **NASA** test pilot, Joe Walker, flew the Landing Research Vehicle that was used to train astronauts for Moon landings. The vehicle used the lift from a jet engine to simulate the reduced gravity on the Moon. Joe Walker also tried out the high speed X-15 rocket plane.

FLYING WINGS

A flying wing is the term given to an aircraft that has practically no fuselage and no tail surfaces. Flying wing designs are attractive and sleek but they are difficult to fly and balance.

An aircraft's wings help lift it from the ground. The fuselage, where the pilot, crew, and passengers sit and where cargo is stored, is heavy. The fuselage weighs an aircraft down and contributes to **drag**. The tail is used to balance the aircraft and also produces drag. If you could design an aircraft with everything inside the wing, it would, designers thought, have less drag and air resistance. The designers were wrong. Despite its beauty, it is difficult to balance a flying wing. The wing needs to be shaped differently from a conventional wing in order to give the required balance and stability.

YB-49
The YB-49 experimental bomber had eight jet engines. It had problems staying stable and one crashed, killing everyone on board. The other YB-49 was destroyed during a high speed run on the ground, which proves that flying wings are difficult to balance.

HORTEN FLYING WINGS
The Horten Ho 229 was a flying wing fighter developed in Germany during World War II. It was test flown first as a glider and then later with two jet engines. It was never flown in combat.

Lifting Body
The X-24 is the complete opposite to a flying wing. The X-24 has almost no wing at all. Known as a "lifting body" aircraft, its fuselage is shaped to provide lift. X-24s are used for flying high in Earth's **atmosphere**.

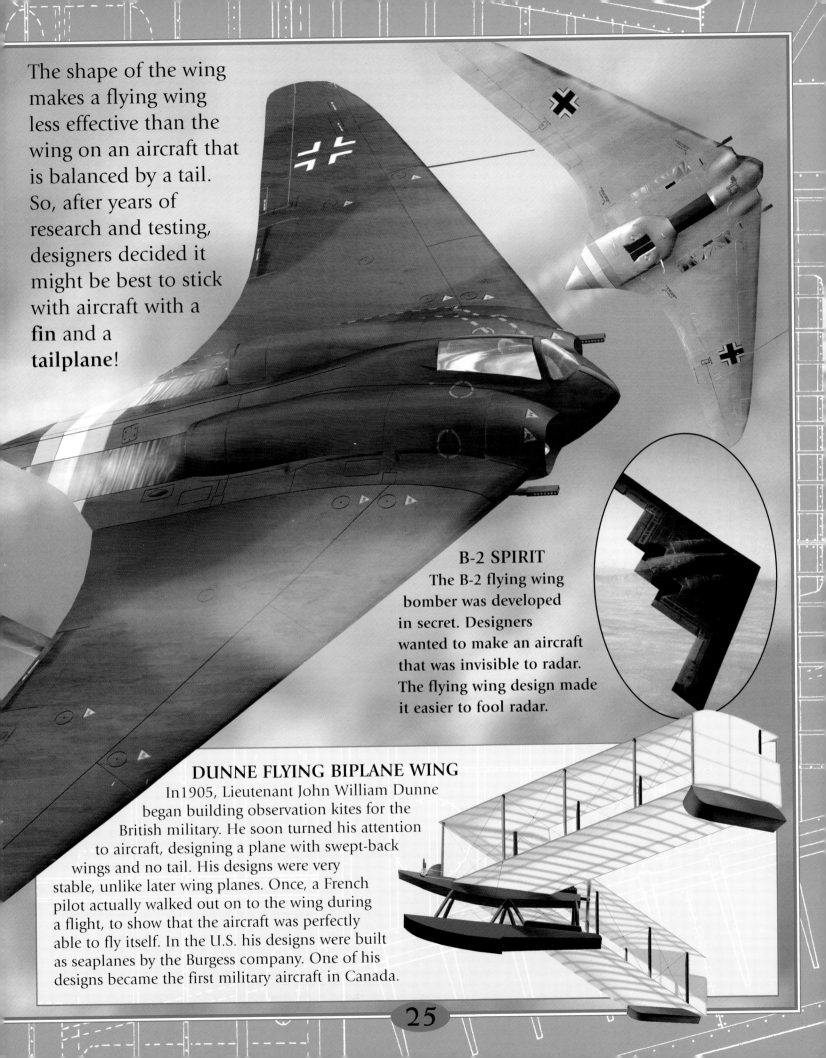

The shape of the wing makes a flying wing less effective than the wing on an aircraft that is balanced by a tail. So, after years of research and testing, designers decided it might be best to stick with aircraft with a **fin** and a **tailplane**!

B-2 SPIRIT
The B-2 flying wing bomber was developed in secret. Designers wanted to make an aircraft that was invisible to radar. The flying wing design made it easier to fool radar.

DUNNE FLYING BIPLANE WING
In 1905, Lieutenant John William Dunne began building observation kites for the British military. He soon turned his attention to aircraft, designing a plane with swept-back wings and no tail. His designs were very stable, unlike later wing planes. Once, a French pilot actually walked out on to the wing during a flight, to show that the aircraft was perfectly able to fly itself. In the U.S. his designs were built as seaplanes by the Burgess company. One of his designs became the first military aircraft in Canada.

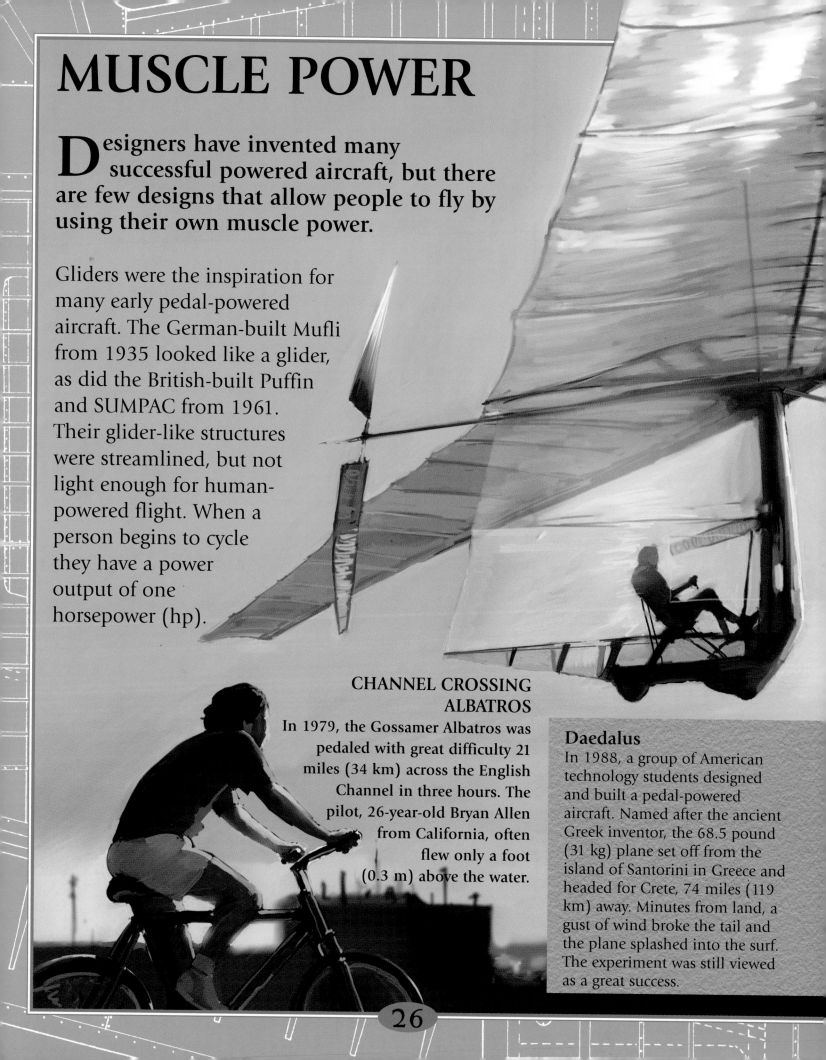

MUSCLE POWER

Designers have invented many successful powered aircraft, but there are few designs that allow people to fly by using their own muscle power.

Gliders were the inspiration for many early pedal-powered aircraft. The German-built Mufli from 1935 looked like a glider, as did the British-built Puffin and SUMPAC from 1961. Their glider-like structures were streamlined, but not light enough for human-powered flight. When a person begins to cycle they have a power output of one horsepower (hp).

CHANNEL CROSSING ALBATROS

In 1979, the Gossamer Albatros was pedaled with great difficulty 21 miles (34 km) across the English Channel in three hours. The pilot, 26-year-old Bryan Allen from California, often flew only a foot (0.3 m) above the water.

Daedalus

In 1988, a group of American technology students designed and built a pedal-powered aircraft. Named after the ancient Greek inventor, the 68.5 pound (31 kg) plane set off from the island of Santorini in Greece and headed for Crete, 74 miles (119 km) away. Minutes from land, a gust of wind broke the tail and the plane splashed into the surf. The experiment was still viewed as a great success.

After a few minutes this output falls to around 0.5 hp, even with a trained athlete. Many small model aircraft engines produce more power than that! Human-powered aircraft do not have to be as streamlined as gliders.

The U.S.-built Gossamer pedal-powered aircraft of the 1970s worked because they were built to be very light. Bracing wires meant they had a lot of drag, but drag matters very little at low speed. In 1977, the Gossamer Condor managed to fly a figure eight, a world's first for human-powered aircraft.

ELECTRIC PENGUIN
In 1980, the Gossamer Penguin was the first aircraft to fly on solar power alone. The Penguin was a scaled down Albatros, piloted by Janice Brown. She weighed only 99 lbs (45 kgs). As with other Gossamer aircraft, a light pilot and airframe were the key to success.

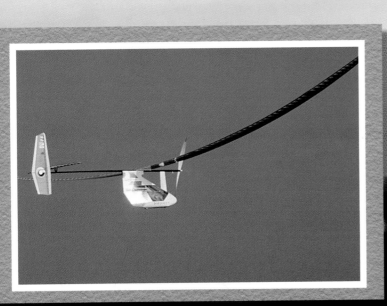

27

CANARDS

An aircraft with the tailplane and elevator at the front is called a canard, which means "duck" in French. Experiments with canards have led to some efficient, high performance aircraft.

PROTEUS
Burt Rutan's Proteus twin jet is designed to operate for up to eighteen hours at 60,000 feet (18,288 meters). It can collect intelligence and environmental data, or relay television signals and communications.

Dick Rutan and Jeana Yeager
A non-stop flight around the world, without refueling, has only ever been made by one aircraft — the canard Voyager. Dick Rutan and Jeana Yeager flew from California to California in 1986. The flight lasted nine days, three minutes, and 44 seconds. The crew had a compartment the size of a phone booth. The Voyager was designed especially for the flight by Dick's brother, Burt Rutan, who also designed the Long-Ez, Beechcraft Starship, and other futuristic canards.

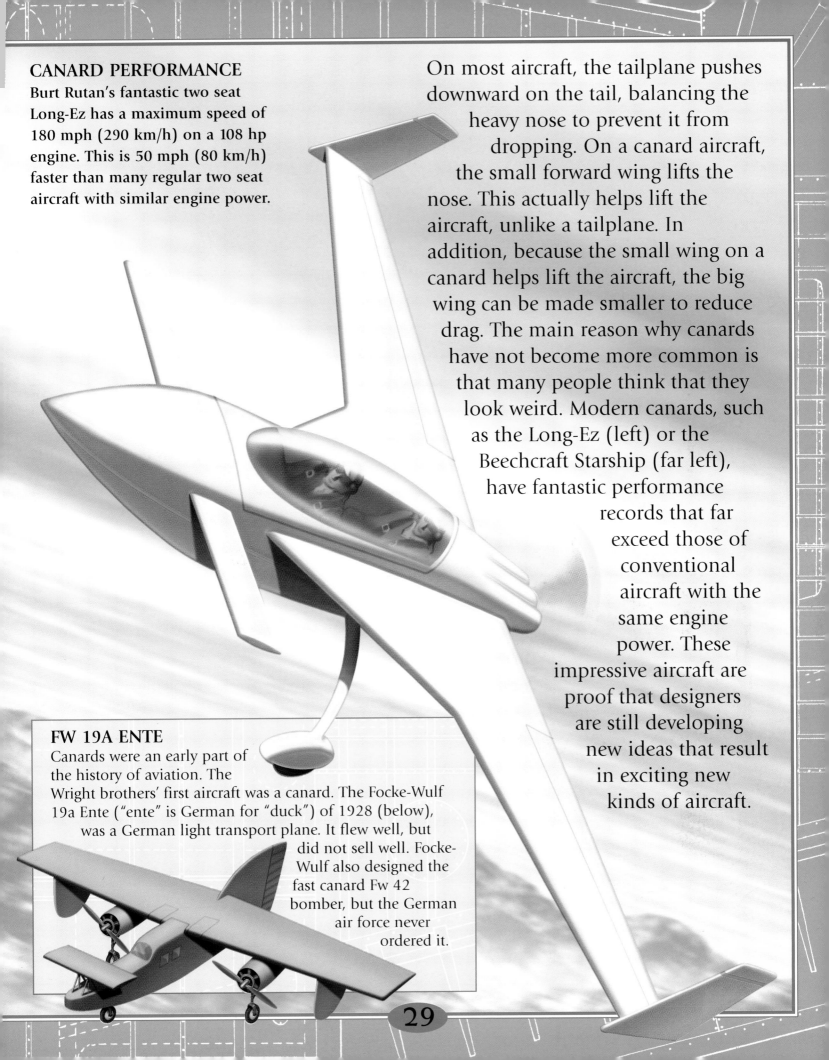

CANARD PERFORMANCE
Burt Rutan's fantastic two seat Long-Ez has a maximum speed of 180 mph (290 km/h) on a 108 hp engine. This is 50 mph (80 km/h) faster than many regular two seat aircraft with similar engine power.

On most aircraft, the tailplane pushes downward on the tail, balancing the heavy nose to prevent it from dropping. On a canard aircraft, the small forward wing lifts the nose. This actually helps lift the aircraft, unlike a tailplane. In addition, because the small wing on a canard helps lift the aircraft, the big wing can be made smaller to reduce drag. The main reason why canards have not become more common is that many people think that they look weird. Modern canards, such as the Long-Ez (left) or the Beechcraft Starship (far left), have fantastic performance records that far exceed those of conventional aircraft with the same engine power. These impressive aircraft are proof that designers are still developing new ideas that result in exciting new kinds of aircraft.

FW 19A ENTE
Canards were an early part of the history of aviation. The Wright brothers' first aircraft was a canard. The Focke-Wulf 19a Ente ("ente" is German for "duck") of 1928 (below), was a German light transport plane. It flew well, but did not sell well. Focke-Wulf also designed the fast canard Fw 42 bomber, but the German air force never ordered it.

SPOTTERS' GUIDE

There is only room for the nose of the mighty HK-1 "Spruce Goose" on these pages, and the Goblin fighter looks very small in contrast. These weird and wonderful aircraft illustrate the extremes in our attempts at creating new or better aircraft. The Condor flies so slowly that you can run beside it, while the XB-70 could fly from London to Paris in just four minutes! Who knows how fast the Caproni Ca-60 would have flown if it had not crashed on its first flight?

ROE TRIPLANE
Length: 23 ft (7 m)
Wingspan: 29 ft 5 in (9 m)
Speed: 19 mph (30 km/h)

**MCDONNELL
XF-85 GOBLIN**
Length: 14 ft 1 in (4.3 m)
Wingspan: 21ft 1 in (6.4 m)
Speed: 650 mph (1,047 km/h)

**HK-1 HERCULES
"SPRUCE GOOSE"**
Length: 218 ft 8 in (66.6 m)
Wingspan: 319 ft 11 in (97.5 m)
Speed: 230 mph (370 km/h)
(estimated)

**"SPRUCE GOOSE" AND
GOSSAMER CONDOR TO
THE SAME SCALE**

NASA
20001

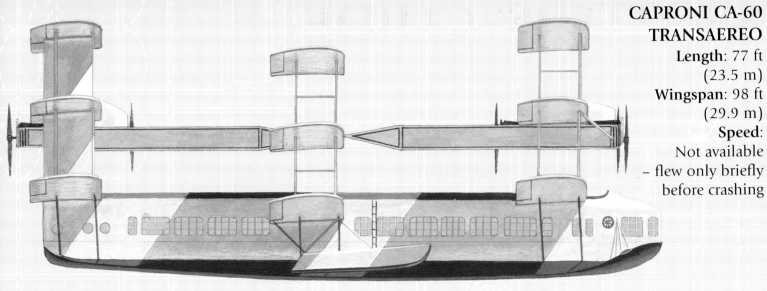

CAPRONI CA-60 TRANSAEREO
Length: 77 ft (23.5 m)
Wingspan: 98 ft (29.9 m)
Speed: Not available – flew only briefly before crashing

BEECHCRAFT STARSHIP
Length: 46 ft 1 in (14 m)
Wingspan: 54 ft 5 in (16.6 m)
Speed: 385 mph (620 km/h)

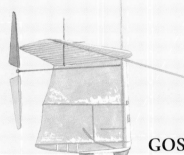

GOSSAMER CONDOR
Length: 31 ft (9.5 m)
Wingspan: 95 ft (29 m)
Speed: 11 mph (17.7 km/h)

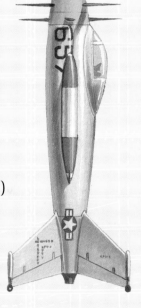

LOCKHEED XFV-1
Length: 37 ft 6 in (11.4 m)
Wingspan: 27 ft 5 in (8.4 m)
Speed: 580 mph (934 km/h) (estimated)

XB-70 'VALKYRIE'
Length: 192 ft 2 in (58.6 m)
Wingspan: 105 ft (32 m)
Speed: 2,056 mph (3,310 km/h)

U.S. AIR FORCE

INDEX

GLOSSARY

ASYMMETRICAL Something that is not balanced or even.

ATMOSPHERE The environment that surrounds and protects Earth.

AUTOGYRO An aircraft powered by a propeller with a horizontal rotor that gives it lift. It looks like a cross between a helicopter and an aircraft.

BRACED Something that is held, fastened, or reinforced.

COLD WAR Political tension and military rivalry that existed mainly between the U.S. and the Soviet Union from the end of World War II until the early 1990s.

CONTRA-ROTATING Spinning in a different or opposite direction.

DRAG The resistance exerted on a moving object that slows it down.

ENGINEER A person who uses science and math to design, build, and operate machines and systems.

FIN An airfoil used to make an aircraft or missile stable during flight.

FUSELAGE The main body of an airplane where the pilot, crew, and passengers are located.

INNOVATIVE Something new, or introduced for the first time.

INTERCONTINENTAL MISSILE Powerful propelled missile that can travel great distances and be launched in one continent and exploded in another.

KOREAN WAR A war from 1950 to 1953 between North Korea aided by China, and South Korea aided by United Nations forces that were mostly U.S. troops.

NASA Stands for the National Aeronautics and Space Administration, the American organization responsible for space flight and exploration.

NAVIGATION The planning, recording, controlling, and charting of a course for a ship or an aircraft.

PARASITE FIGHTER A fighter aircraft fixed to a larger one.

RECONNAISSANCE Exploration of an area made by the military to gain information.

SOVIET UNION The Union of Soviet Socialist Republics, a group of countries that were under communist rule from 1922 to 1991.

SUPERSONIC Faster than the speed of sound.

TAILPLANE Rear portion of the fuselage that stabilizes it.

TRAPEZE A short horizontal bar suspended from the bottom of an aircraft.

TRENCH A deep ditch used to hide and protect soldiers, especially in World War I.

U-BOAT A submarine of the German navy (from unterseeboot).

VIETNAM WAR A war from 1963 to 1975 between North Vietnam aided by the Soviet Union, and South Vietnam aided by the United States.

WORLD WAR I A war fought from 1914 to 1918 in which Great Britain, France, Russia, Canada, the United States and other allies defeated Germany and Austria.

WORLD WAR II A war from 1939 to 1945 in which Great Britain, France, the Soviet Union, the United States, and other allies defeated Germany, Italy, and Japan.